TRENGWAINTON GARDEN

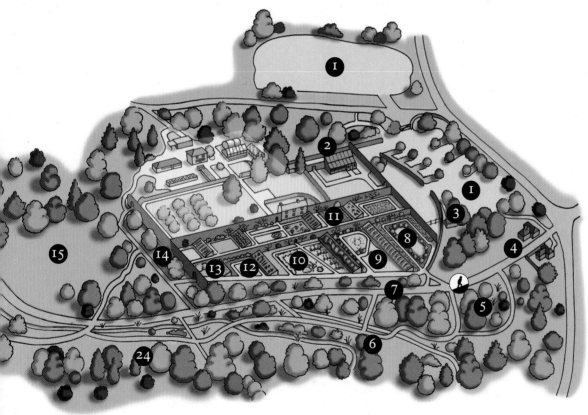

National Trust

Trengwainton Garden

Trengwainton is the answer to a gardener's prayers, where the rhododendrons start flowering in November and magnolias in February. The name is Cornish for 'the settlement of spring' – a reference to the early vernal beauty of this favoured part of Penwith. This area of Cornwall also gets about 120cm (50in) of rain a year. So the soil – an acid, medium loam – is always moist. Thanks to the Gulf Stream and the sheltered position looking south over Mount's Bay, the climate is exceptionally mild and so plants will grow here almost all year round. Indeed, you will find tender exotics at Trengwainton that won't survive elsewhere on the British mainland.

The garden is long and thin, flanking a drive that winds uphill towards the house. At the bottom, unusual plants from four continents fill a range of walled gardens. At the top, you can stop and take in broad views out over the bay to St Michael's Mount and the Lizard Peninsula.

Rhododendron 'Golden Oriole'

Sir Rose Price and the Birth of the Garden

Since at least the 16th century, there has been a dwelling at Trengwainton. It belonged to the great West Country family of Arundell during the 18th century.

In 1814 Trengwainton was bought by Rose Price, the son of a wealthy Jamaican sugar planter. A year later he was created a baronet and immediately began to make improvements to the house. He planted trees on a considerable scale – mainly beech, ash and sycamore, some of which are still standing – principally around the house and on both sides of a new drive now known as the Long Walk. He also built a series of brick-walled gardens at the foot of the drive with highly unusual raised sloping beds for growing early produce.

Sir Rose Price died in 1834, the year after William Wilberforce's Emancipation Act had freed the slaves on the Worthy Park estate in Jamaica from which he derived his income. So in 1836 Price's heirs sold Trengwainton to pay off his debts.

The Bolithos – A Family of Plantsmen

In 1867 the property was bought by T.S. Bolitho, a banker descended from an ancient Cornish family which had been involved in Cornish mining for many generations. It was his son, Thomas Robins Bolitho, who in 1897 enlarged the house to its present size and built the wide carriage drive leading down to the Lodge.

When T.R. Bolitho died in 1925, Trengwainton passed to his nephew, Lt Col Edward Bolitho. After retiring from the Army, he quickly made his mark on Cornish life, serving as High Sheriff, County Alderman, Lord Lieutenant and Chairman of the County Council. He was knighted in 1952. Sir Edward Bolitho transformed the garden, ably assisted by his head gardener, Alfred Creek, who was a first-class propagator. Mr Creek had been appointed in 1904, but it was not until Lt Col Bolitho's arrival in 1925 that he was given the opportunity to demonstrate his exceptional talent. Three great Cornish gardeners, J.C. Williams of Caerhays, P.D. Williams of Lanarth and Canon A.T. Boscawen of Ludgvan, helped not only with advice, but with gifts of rhododendrons and other shrubs. The only rhododendrons in the garden of an earlier date, apart from great thickets of *R. ponticum* in the woods near the house, were the *R. falconeri* and *griffithianum* planted in 1904.

Thomas Simon Bolitho and his wife Elizabeth. They bought Trengwainton in 1867 and built the carriage drive through the garden

Rhododendron 'Cornish Red'

The Terrace Walk in 1866. St Michael's Mount is visible in the distance

Bluebells, azaleas and tree ferns in the Lower Stream Garden

Bringing New Plants to Trengwainton

In 1926 G.H. Johnstone of Trewithen and Lawrence Johnston of Hidcote Manor in Gloucestershire offered Lt Col Bolitho a share in Frank Kingdon-Ward's 1927–8 plant-hunting expedition to north-east Assam and the Mishmi Hills in upper Burma. It was from seed gathered by Kingdon-Ward that the rhododendron collection at Trengwainton was largely established, and it was due to Mr Creek's skill that these very tender seedlings were so successfully raised. *Rhododendron macabeanum*, *R. elliottii*, *R. taggianum* and *R. concatenans* flowered here for the first time in the British Isles. Most of Kingdon-Ward's rhododendrons were planted in the shelter of the plantations, and Lt Col Bolitho used several of the walled gardens in which to establish many other tender species. His other major project of the 1920s was to open up the stream beside the drive, which had previously run through an underground culvert.

Opening the Garden

On 24 May 1931 Lt Col Bolitho opened the garden for the first time, noting in his diary that 'hundreds came and the conduct of the people was entirely satisfactory'. In 1934 Mr Creek retired, to be succeeded as head gardener by G.W. Thomas, who came from the home of Sir William Lawrence, late President of the Royal Horticultural Society. He was a skilled hybridiser and, with Lt Col Bolitho, made a number of successful new rhododendron crosses. In 1938, Trengwainton was by far the most successful exhibitor at the RHS Rhododendron Show in London.

The Wartime Garden

During the Second World War, the shrubs were neglected, as the garden was given over to food production. 2,500lb of tomatoes were grown in the open in 1941, and the tennis court and lawn were ploughed and cropped with potatoes, leeks, onions and cucumbers – over 5 tons of these were sold in 1944 – while thousands of lettuces were grown in the Walled Gardens. Three land girls and two boys worked full-time in the garden in 1943, earning 38 shillings (£1.90) per week.

Trengwainton in Recent Years

George Hulbert became Head Gardener after the war and was in charge when the Stream Garden was planted up with masses of primulas and other moisture-loving plants. He was succeeded by Nigel Marshall and then by Peter Horder. The present Head Gardener, Ian Wright, trained at the Royal Horticultural Society's Wisley Garden and worked at The Vyne and Tresco Abbey Gardens in the early part of his career.

In recognition of Sir Edward's achievements at Trengwainton, the Royal Horticultural Society awarded him the coveted Victoria Medal of Honour for Horticulture in 1961. In the same year he generously gave the property to the National Trust together with the surrounding estate, 98 acres (39.7 hectares) in all. With this gift, Sir Edward provided a substantial endowment and arranged for the garden to be opened to the public. Following Sir Edward's death in 1969, Trengwainton was occupied by his son Simon, who, as well as a career in banking,

Giant Echium pininana abound throughout the garden

learnt to fly in the 1930s, then served first in the Navy before thirteen years in the Army, ending his life as an Honorary Air Commodore in the Royal Air Force. He was another knowledgeable plantsman and gardener who had a great influence on Trengwainton, constructing the Jubilee Garden in 1977 and Prince William Walk in 1982.

Simon Bolitho was succeeded at his death in 1991 by his son, Colonel Edward Bolitho OBE who maintains an active interest in the National Trust's management of the garden. He and his family now live in the house and we would ask that you please respect their privacy.

After 40 years of ownership, the National Trust is developing the garden to increase visitor interest and enjoyment, including the gradual restoration of the Walled Kitchen Garden.

Lt Col Sir Edward and Lady Bolitho

The greenhouses above the Walled Gardens enabled Trengwainton to produce a huge range of tender vegetables

Tour of the Garden

You are free to follow any of the many routes through the garden, but the circuit suggested here visits all the main areas and takes in the major features and plants of special interest.

The Stream Garden to the south of the Drive

Candelabra primulas in the Stream Garden

1 Car-park

2 Tea room
Established in 2001, this garden with its lawn and wall borders contains the tea room which was designed along environmentally friendly principles to take advantage of seasonal sunlight.

3 Toilets

4 Reception, shop and plant sales
The Lodge containing the shop was built in 1994, matching the original Lodge built around 1820. Beside the Lodges are some Chinese Chusan Fan palms (*Trachycarpus fortunei*). A vibant red, May-flowering *Rhododendron* x 'Leo' gives interest after the large *Magnolia* x *loebneri* 'Merrill' has finished flowering. In front of the old lodge is *Camellia japonica* 'Debbie', which is a large double red, the plant bowing over with the weight of its flowers when it is in full bloom.

Turn left into the Jubilee Garden.

5 Jubilee Garden
Known in the 19th century as the Vineyard, this garden was created to commemorate the Queen's Silver Jubilee in 1977. On the left of the entrance is a magnificent *Magnolia campbellii* 'Kew's Surprise'. Look out for its unusual red seed pods in October. Opposite is the semi-herbaceous *Impatiens tinctoria*, the giant busy lizzie. Its seeds are dispersed when the pods explode outwards in summer. Other plants of note are the spiky-leafed acanthus, a fine example of *Rhododendron sinogrande* and *Idesia polycarpa*, with its heart-shaped leaves. *Clerodendrum trichotomum* var. *fargesii* fills the garden with its fragrance during late summer.

After passing a Dianella tasmanica, *which has vivid purple-blue fruits in late summer, you enter a tunnel of bamboo that leads through to the Tree Fern Glade. A slight detour to your right will allow you to rest a while in the Laurel Circle.*

6 Tree Fern Glade
On the far side of the stream, large-leaved plants predominate: the rounded-leaves of *Petasites japonicus* var. *giganteus* mix with the upright leaves of *Lysichiton americanus*, the bog arum or 'skunk cabbage'. Near the path is Rhododendron 'Johnnie Johnston', which was raised in the garden in 1944. Its unusual pink flowers are heavily scented. On both sides of the stream and path is a grove of tree ferns – *Dicksonia antarctica* – from Tasmania, which seed themselves freely on the surrounding banks and walls. Also here you will find the more tender *Dicksonia fibrosa*. These are complemented by the large white-flowered *Rhododendron yunnanense*. Turning right, after the bridge, the Lower Well can be found, known locally as 'Manny James' Well, but we have yet to discover why!

Turn right again on to the Lower Drive.

A grove of tree ferns (*Dicksonia antarctica*) towers over the Stream Garden. In the centre is *Chamaecyparis lawsoniana* 'Intertexta'

7 Lower Drive

Looking up the Lower Drive, beyond the *Rhododendron loderi* with its large leaves and highly scented white flowers in the spring, you will see a tall fir – *Chamaecyparis lawsoniana* 'Intertexta'. This towers over a *R. vernicosum* hybrid, whose cascading flowers look particularly good in late spring. To its left is a *Ginkgo biloba*, the Maidenhair Tree, the oldest living species of tree. Some specimens are more than a thousand years old. Herbal remedies made from this plant have a miraculous reputation as an anti-ageing tonic and can speed up mental reactions and improve short-term memory. Elsewhere on the Lower Drive is a selection of *R. arboreum* and of Abutilons, which do extremely well in the garden, flowering almost throughout the year.

A short distance back down the drive, a green gate heralds the entrance to the Walled Gardens.

The Walled Gardens

Above the gate is a large *Davidia involucrata*, or Hankerchief Tree, covered in spectacular white bracts in late spring. The Walled Gardens, some four acres (1.6 hectares) in size, were built around 1814 to provide fruit, vegetables and flowers for all those who lived at Trengwainton. Brick walls are unusual in this part of the country; the materials to build them had to be imported in two shiploads from Somerset, with a kiln being set up near the garden to fire the bricks.

In Trengwainton's mild climate, the magnolias in the Walled Garden have grown to their full size

8 Veitchii Garden

Lieutenant Colonel Edward Bolitho had this walled garden cleared in 1937. It had been a wilderness for many years, and was then cleaned with a crop of potatoes before becoming a shrub garden. For many years it was known as 'The Colonel's Corner'.

This garden is dominated by a fine specimen of *Magnolia* x *veitchii* 'Peter Veitch', planted in 1936. This fast-growing hybrid of *M. campbellii* and *M. denudata*, raised by a well-known Exeter nurseryman, bears masses of white flowers, flushed with pink, in April. Behind it is one of the original *Metasequoia glyptostroboides*, grown from seed in 1947. This ancient tree was thought to be extinct, being found only in fossils. Then, in the 1940s, living specimens were found in China, and this tree was grown from some of their first seed brought back to England. Next to it is the unusual *Rehderodendron macrocarpum* from China, whose white cherry-like flowers appear in late spring. Behind is a fine *Drimys winteri*, an evergreen discovered in Tierra del Fuego by Capt. William Winter, one of Sir Francis Drake's commanders on his voyage round the world. It is said that he boiled the leaves and gave the tea to his crew to prevent scurvy. Beyond is a white-flowered *Magnolia campbellii alba*, and on the west side of this garden are a number of azaras from Chile including the yellow-flowered *Azara dentata*, as well as a wall of camellias planted in 1941 and a large example of *Eucalyptus subcrenulata* from Tasmania, one of the hardiest in this climate. The top of this garden is one of the mildest spots where some of the more tender species overwinter, such as banksia, melaleuca, grevillea and correa.

The Walled Garden from the Colonel's Corner

The Lower Drive in the 19th century

9

9 Campbellii Garden

Near the entrance to the next garden is a magnificent example of *M. campbellii*, planted as a five-year-old tree in 1926. The large, cup-shaped, rose-pink flowers, paler within, are a handsome sight in early February and March, although, being the first magnolia to flower, there is always the risk of frost damage. Behind and beyond that is another *Drimys winteri*. A tender, finely shaped *Michelia doltsopa*, a relative of the magnolia, is covered with sweetly scented white flowers in May. The south-facing border at the top of this garden has at its eastern end a fine example of *Stewartia sinensis*, a tree with an attractive peeling red-brown bark and white flowers in late summer. Near the unusual schefflera or umbrella tree is the black tree fern *Cyathea dealbata*.

10 Middle Walled Garden

This was originally named after Mr G. W. Thomas, Lt Col Bolitho's Head Gardener from 1934 to 1946, but now referred to as the Middle Walled Garden and has a good form of *Magnolia mollicomata* near the entrance. A *Pseudopanax laetus* with its waxy leaves ison the left of the centre path. Beyond, a group of *Euphorbia mellifera* smells strongly of honey when in flower. Also in the centre bed is a *Eucryphia cordifolia* from Chile, a *Magnolia sprengeri* var. *diva* planted in 1958, a *M.* x *wieseneri* from Japan, another *Michelia doltsopa* and an old *Enkianthus chinensis*. Nearer to the green door is one of the best *Magnolia cylindrica* in the country, whose branches

The spreading branches of a mature *Magnolia campbellii*

are covered in a mass of upright narrow white flowers in April. On the north wall some tall acacia trees grow, covered in yellow flowers in early spring, while the narrow border on the west wall houses a number of tender scented rhododendrons.

Heading through the green door, you reach the Kitchen Garden.

11 Kitchen Garden

These five sections were built to the dimensions of Noah's Ark – 300 cubits long by 50 cubits wide, a cubit being about 45cm

The pink petals of *Magnolia campbellii* carpet the ground in the spring among clumps of *Leucojum vernum*

The sloping beds in the Kitchen Garden were built to grow early vegetables, fruit and flowers

(17in), or the span of a man's lower arm. Directly ahead of you is the Head Gardener's Cottage which is built into the north wall. Turning left and heading to the farthest garden you will find a viewing platform. From here you can see most clearly the unique raised, sloping beds that characterise these gardens. Designed for the cultivation of early vegetables, fruit and flowers, they probably show how the climate changed in the 19th century. Following the cold weather of most of the 17th and 18th centuries – known to climatologists as the Little Ice Age – the weather between 1790 and 1809 was much milder. However, several cold winters followed. We originally believed Sir Rose Price built these beds, because he feared that the cold weather had returned, but the latest findings point towards a global drop in temperature caused by the eruption of Mt Tambora in Indonesia and its ensuing ash cloud.

By the pond is a large *Osmunda regalis* or Royal Fern, well over 100 years old and growing over an old rock garden. The fibrous rootstock of this species is the source of osmunda fibre, used as potting compost for orchids. The pond was originally a 'dipping pond', from which the garden was watered before hoses were easily available. Beside it are old moulds in which tin ingots were made at the Bolitho smelting works in Chyandour on the edge of Penzance in the 19th century. The central area is now used as a seasonal cut-flower garden. We will be gradually reintroducing fruit and vegetables to all five walled sections as funding permits.

Returning back to the Middle Walled Garden, we next come to the Fuchsia Garden.

Daffodils fill the Meadow in spring

12 Fuchsia Garden

The sloping eastern border contains *Coriaria terminalis* var. *xanthocarpa*, a handsome perennial with arching, frond-like leaves and striking clusters of translucent fruits, as well as cordylines or Cabbage Palms, eryngiums, yucca and various tender fuchsias. It is from the many different fuchsias which flower almost throughout the year that this garden takes its name. They range from the tiny *F. microphylla* and the *F. procumbens*, climbing the sloping bed by the entrance, to a number of unusual tender varieties and the very large, orange-barked tree *Fuchsia excorticata*, from New Zealand, which has edible fruits. Look out for the *Fuchsia coccinea*, which has now climbed to the top of the athrotaxis (tall fir) by the entrance to the Foliage Garden.

13 Foliage Garden

This garden was re-landscaped in 2001 and has been planted with additional tender foliage plants. This will maintain the Trengwainton tradition of experimentation, where the new plants will join established residents such as *Illicium simonsii*, the banana plant *Musa basjoo*, the Lily of the Valley tree from Madeira, *Pseudopanax ferox* with its sword-like leaves, and several *Tetrapanax papyrifer*. The bower on the south wall of the garden was cut out of the large *Podocarpus acutifolius* in 1993. A small patch of the vivid blue flowering *Myostidium hortensia* has been planted, the common name being Chatham Island Forget-me-nots. The stone troughs in this garden are bedded out with succulents in the summer and bulbs in the spring. To the right of the gate, just before you leave this section, is the waxy-flowered *Lapageria* 'Flesh Pink' Penhale.

Camellia japonica 'Magnoliiflora'

14 Camellia Walk

In 1939 Lt Col Bolitho planted a large number of new and seedling *Camellia japonica* and *Camellia* x *williamsii* – named after the Williams family of Caerhays in east Cornwall – along the western wall of the Walled Gardens. Directly opposite the gate is *Rhaphiolepis umbellata*, the white-flowered evergreen shrub. Halfway up the walk on the left is an *Acer palmatum* 'Heptalobum Elegans'.

Returning to the drive and heading uphill, you reach the Meadow on your right.

15 The Meadow

The large Common Oak (*Quercus robur*) was planted to commemorate Queen Victoria's Diamond Jubilee in 1897. Near it is a species of lime, *Tilia platyphyllos*, planted in 1901 to mark the coronation of King Edward VII. The Queen Mother planted the *Pinus wallichiana* close to the drive in 1962. The upper side of the Meadow contains a layer of the original plant of the yellow-flowered *Rhododendron macabeanum*. This received the RHS first-class certificate in 1938, with Trengwainton being the first garden to see it flower since it was collected during anexpedition by Frank Kingdon-Ward in 1972.

Right at the back of the Meadow is a fine example of *Magnolia campbellii* 'Caerhays Belle', which makes a magnificent sight in April when it is covered in huge pink flowers. The purple *Acer palmatum atropurpureum* stands next to a *Magnolia stellata* at the top end of the Meadow by the drive. Both are overshadowed by a large *Magnolia campbellii*.

Magnolia campbellii

The Stream Garden

16 Stream Garden and Drive

Just across the drive is the main Stream Garden, which provides colour throughout the spring and summer, and was opened in the 1920s by Lt Col Bolitho. It makes a favourable site for moisture-loving plants such as *Primula helodoxa* (the Candelabra Primula) and the purplish-red *P. japonica*, *Mimulus luteus*, *Polygonum campanulatum* and various crocosmia, astilbes and zantedschia (Arum Lily) and hedychiums. On the other side of the drive is a variety of shrubs including the locally raised *Cornus capitata* 'Madron', and the flowers of the bulbs of *Nerine bowdenii* which provide colour in the late autumn.

The rhododendron flowering season starts early in November with *R. nobleanum*, then *R.* 'Christmas Cheer'. Examples of the tall self-sown *Echium pininana*, from Madeira, abound here and elsewhere in the garden. Providing the previous winter has not been too cold, they can send up towers of blue flowers up to four metres in height.

In the field beyond the park fencing is a clump of the Monterey Pine, *Pinus radiata*, a prominent feature in the landscape of west Cornwall and very tolerant of the strong, salt-laden winds.

A path now leads off the drive towards the Upper Pond and Bridge.

17 Upper Pond and Bridge

Passing half of an old millstone, you will see the large rhododendrons, 'Creeks Cross', which are named after Trengwainton's renowned Head Gardener, Alfred Creek. Also note the skin-like bark of the rhododendron from the shilsonii group. Crossing the Long Walk, you come to the pond created in 1997. Some of the old tree ferns around the pond were moved into new positions, with surprising ease. The lower path leads into a glade, an area which is planted with a mixture of different ferns and grasses.

As you leave the Glade, you will see a dipping well, which was discovered when the area was cleared. As there is another well just a few metres away in the Azalea Garden, it may be that this dried up, and that a new one had to be dug to provide a reliable water supply to the house.

18 House Lawn

From the House Lawn there are fine views to the south front of Trengwainton House. The lawn is flanked by summer-flowering mixed borders originally designed by the late Graham Stuart Thomas, the eminent gardener and author.

19 Trengwainton House (private)

The house has undergone considerable alterations over the years and was extensively remodelled in 1897. It is still lived in by members of the Bolitho family and is not open to the public. We would therefore ask you to respect their privacy.

20 Ha-ha

Care is needed near this sudden drop, which is used to give the impression of an unbroken expanse of lawn without fencing.

21 Terrace

Approached through some *Pinus radiata*, with a view to the Summer-houses, this area and its surrounding shelter of trees takes the brunt of the prevailing south-westerly winds and is crucial for the protection of the rest of the garden. It was devastated by the storms of January 1990, when nearly all the Holm Oak (*Quercus ilex*) that had arched over the terrace for well over 100 years came down. However, replanting took place, and in the Cornish climate the replacements – a mixture of *Quercus ilex*, beech, ash, turkey oak and alder – have grown extremely quickly. From the Terrace there are wonderful views to the Lizard Peninsula, St Michael's Mount and the fishing village of Newlyn. Below the Terrace wall, framed in agapanthus from Tresco, a large slate toposcope, or direction finder, now dominates the lawn. The carvings created by local artist Joe Hemming represent the traditional industry, wildlife and legends of the area and are: the *Lizard* – represents Lizard Head, the most southerly point of England; *Lamb and Flag* – the tin-smelting mark of the Bolithos in the 18th

and 19th centuries; *Mermaid* – depicts the mermaid carved in the church at Zennor; *Bird* – a Woodcock which winters in the deep sheltered valleys; *Miner's Shovel* – commemorates the ancient tin-mining industry of Cornwall; *Pilchards* – the Bolitho family exported these fish from this area in the 18th century; *Scythe* – honours the local farmers and their traditions; *Fishing Boat* – represents the Newlyn and Cornish fishing industry.

During March and April a small path is open which leads from the Terrace to the Magnolia Garden which has champion examples of *Magnolia sargentiana* var. *robusta* and *Magnolia delavayi*.

Returning across the House Lawn, and this time taking the upper route at the fork in the path, you reach the Azalea Garden, via another grove of tree ferns, planted in 1931.

Below left Pieris formosa var. *forrestii*, white-flowered with pink bracts next to the drive

Below right Candelabra primulas in the Stream Garden

22 Azalea Garden or Ation Alley

In the spring you will be greeted by a group of '-ation' Camellias, including 'Anticipation', 'Citation', 'Donation', 'Exaltation', 'Innovation', 'Inspiration', 'Jubilation' and 'Salutation'. This garden takes its name from the planting of fragrant azaleas that provide a splash of colour in May. Further uphill is a fine specimen of *Cryptomeria japonica* 'Elegans' and a large *Rhododendron arboreum* 'Cornish Red'. The path then leads through old laurels and past a number of myrtles, *Luma apiculata*, with their orange trunks and white flowers in the summer, and several late-flowering *R.* 'Polar Bear', with white flowers in July. Heading downhill, you will reach the pond once again, passing the large stems of the heavily scented *R.* 'Loderi King George'.

Go straight on and walk down the Long Walk.

23 Long Walk

This was the main drive until T. R. Bolitho built the present road. Local folklore has it that drunken coachmen collecting guests after dinner had been racing one another down the narrow drive and causing too many accidents. It is particularly colourful in summer and autumn, when the swathes of varieties of numerous blue and white hydrangeas are in full flower. Around a third of the way down, on the left-hand side, is a striking stand of the yellow-striped bamboo *Phyllostachys bambusoides* 'Castilloni', while further down is the black bamboo *Phyllostachys nigra*, the colour of which becomes more pronounced as the stronger summer light ripens the canes.

Taking the right fork, you turn into Prince William Walk.

24 Prince William Walk

Created in 1982, this path leads through an exotic-looking Chilean *Podocarpus salignus* to where the stream reappears. Here, water-loving plants provide colour throughout the season and lead to a bridge over a waterfall. Beyond this the area is dominated by clumps of elegantly leaved hostas, delicate epimediums, and two tall trees, a *Sequoia sempervirens* on the right of the path, and a superb specimen of *Cupressus macrocarpa* on the left.

The path then returns to the Tree Fern Glade. A left turn will take you back on to the Lower Drive, tea room, shop and car-park.

Azaleas and bluebells in May